DJs, Ratings, and Hook Tapes

POP MUSIC BROADCASTING

David Hautzig

Macmillan Publishing Company   New York
Maxwell Macmillan Canada   Toronto
Maxwell Macmillan International   New York   Oxford   Singapore   Sydney

Macmillan Publishing Company is part of the Maxwell Communication Group
of Companies.
Macmillan Publishing Company
866 Third Avenue, New York, NY 10022
Maxwell Macmillan Canada, Inc.
1200 Eglinton Avenue East, Suite 200
Don Mills, Ontario M3C 3N1
First edition
Printed in the United States of America

10 9 8 7 6 5 4 3 2 1

The text of this book is set in 12.5 point Meridien.
Book design by Constance Ftera.

Library of Congress Cataloging-in-Publication Data
Hautzig, David R.
    DJs, ratings, and hook tapes : pop music broadcasting / David Hautzig. —
1st ed.
        p.   cm.
    Includes index.
    Summary: Explains what happens behind the scenes at a radio station,
discussing the work of the program director, researchers, production director,
disc jockeys, business manager, and other key figures.
    ISBN 0-02-743471-0
    1. Radio broadcasting—Juvenile literature. 2. Radio—Production and
direction—Juvenile literature. [1. Radio broadcasting. 2. Radio—Production and direction.] I. Title.
PN1991.75.H36 1993   791.44'0232—dc20   91-33588

CONTENTS

To one of the finest people I have ever known, Jon Ross

—D. H.

INTRODUCTION

Before television, radio was an important source of information and entertainment. You didn't *watch* the World Series, you listened to it on the radio. When President Franklin Delano Roosevelt spoke to the country during the Great Depression, people listened to him on the radio. For entertainment, people listened to radio shows like "Flash

Gordon," "Duffy's Tavern," "Inner Sanctum," and "The Shadow."

Today, radio's role is different. People rarely sit down in front of their radio the way they do with their television. People listen to the radio while they do other things: work, make dinner, or drive a car.

Unlike most network and local television, which show a little bit of everything (drama, comedy, news, sports), many radio stations play only one thing. This is called the station's *format*. Some radio stations play only jazz, while others play only classical music. Popular music stations can have even more specific formats. Some play only "golden oldies," while others play a range of current rock and roll. Still others play only hits—songs in the top forty or top one hundred. There are stations that have news twenty-four hours a day. Some stations feature *talk radio* where listeners can call up and talk about any topic from politics to football. So radio has something for just about everybody, just not all on the same station.

To get the information for this book, I went to two radio stations in New York City: WNEW-FM and WHTZ-FM (known as Z-100). In this book, I show the different people and describe the jobs involved in running those stations. The radio stations you listen to may do things a bit differently, but once you understand how WNEW-FM and Z-100 work, you'll have a very good idea of how the average radio station works.

When I listen to the radio, I want to hear music that I know and like. Sometimes I go up and down the dial for ten minutes before I find a song I like. But if I liked every song that a radio station played, chances are somebody else would *hate* every song that same station played. Music radio stations try to please everybody by playing a variety of songs. How does that music actually get on the radio?

It all starts with the latest recordings. The record companies send their products to the *music director,* who is in charge of the *music department.* The music director receives about fifty new recordings each week, along with information about them. That information includes sales figures, which other radio stations are playing the music, and how many people have seen the recording artist in concert. The music director checks that the information from the record companies is accurate. For example, a record company may say a new recording is selling well. The music director then calls a few record stores. If the stores say that sales really are good, the station is more likely to play it.

Before playing songs on the radio, though, most radio stations test them. WNEW tests music by calling people on the telephone, playing some songs for them, and then getting their reactions. This work is done by members of the *research department,* who go through the phone book every day and randomly choose people to call. When the researchers call, they don't say they are calling from a radio station. They simply ask the person if he would like to take part in a music survey. If the person says yes, the researcher asks him what radio stations he listens to. If a person says he listens to a radio station that plays only jazz, chances are he won't know about the new Bruce Springsteen record. If the person says he listens to rock and roll, the research department plays a "hook tape" which lasts about six minutes and contains ten-second segments from about thirty songs, both new and old. Why only ten seconds? "If the person doesn't recognize the song after ten seconds, he doesn't know it," explains one member of WNEW's research department.

The people are asked to rate each song on a scale of one to five, with one being the lowest

rating. After all the calls are finished, the results are put into a computer and analyzed. The music director uses the information from the computer, along with information from the record companies, to decide what to play on the station.

The music director and the *research director* choose the music that goes onto the hook tape.

The music director generally chooses what new music gets tested because he or she got the music from the record companies and is already familiar with it. The research director generally chooses which older songs get tested because he or she knows how long it has been since the song was last tested.

Requests are also important in deciding what gets played on a radio station. What better way to find out what people want to hear than to have them tell you? Radio stations encourage their listeners to call a special telephone number if they want to hear a particular song. Every week, for example, the music departments of both WNEW and Z-100 count how many times a song was requested the previous week.

The people at each radio station also listen to what other stations play. Adam Goodman, the assistant music director at Z-100, says that he listens to the competition every day. "I listen to WNEW regularly because I may hear a new rock and roll song that I think Z-100 should play."

Because Z-100 plays only hits, a lot of the music they play they hear on other stations first. They must listen to the competition. WNEW music director Lorraine Caruso doesn't ignore other stations, either. She tunes into the competition to see if there is something she might have missed.

After narrowing down the choices, the music director recommends what he or she thinks should be played on the radio station to the *program director*. Together, they look at all the information that has been gathered from research, sales information, and requests. Then intuition comes into play. "There are times when somebody has to add some personal opinion to the decision," says Steve Kingston, Z-100's program director.

The program director chooses songs to be played on the station, and they get added to the *playlist*. The playlist is just that: a list of what songs disc jockeys (DJs) can play on the radio station. At a station like WNEW, the playlist can have thousands of songs because any song that is considered rock and roll can be on it. However, the playlist at Z-100 has only about three hundred songs because Z-100 plays only hits.

The music department reports the station's playlist and *rotation* to magazines and newspapers that cover radio. (This is done so that a radio station in Texas or Wyoming can know what WNEW and Z-100 are playing. They may read about a song they have never heard that is very popular in New York, and then add it to *their* playlist.) The rotation refers to how often a song is played. If a song gets played a lot on a station, that song is in heavy rotation. At WNEW, that means three or four times a day. At Z-100, which plays fewer songs, that means every two to three hours.

The music director and the music department also maintain the music library at the radio station. Everything that gets played on a station is saved in the music library in one form or another. All new recordings sent to radio stations are now on compact disc (CD). Older material is still on vinyl records, although many old records have been transferred to compact disc by the record companies. WNEW has around seventy thousand items in its music library. When you consider that the station has been on the air since 1967, it's probably not that surprising. Still, that's a lot of recordings.

THE DISC JOCKEY

After the music department makes all of its decisions, the log goes to the *disc jockey*. Now the music that's been chosen actually goes on the air with the voice of the DJ.

Most people believe a disc jockey's job is the easiest in the world: He plays songs, then talks about them. There is a bit more to it. The DJ's job is to make the station fun and entertaining to listen to.

The typical work shift for a DJ is four hours. Some are only three hours, while others are five or even six hours long. But the average is four. DJs usually get to the station about an hour before the shift starts. They read their mail, check to see if there are any special instructions for that day's show (like a contest for concert tickets), and read the day's newspapers. DJs need to be well informed about current events. They may want to play a song that they think is appropriate for the day. For example, the day Nelson Mandela was set free by the South African government, WNEW played a song by Tracy Chapman written for Mandela while he was in prison.

While on the air, a DJ's most important task is to keep the radio station on schedule. At Z-100, every minute of every day is planned in advance. It is the DJ's job to follow the schedule. He constantly checks the schedule and the clock to see if he is on time. Sometimes things don't go perfectly. The schedule may say that a song by Madonna is to be played at 2:10 P.M. However, the news report right before the song lasted four minutes longer than expected. So now it is 2:14 P.M. and the show is running four minutes long. Somewhere along the line, those four minutes have to be made up. The DJ and program director decide what to do. Since commercials are paid for (more about that later), they can't be taken out of the schedule. Instead, they look for a song that is about four minutes long and take it out. This is called dropping a song. Then the station is back on schedule…for a little while.

The DJs at WNEW also have a schedule to follow, but it isn't as strict as the one at Z-100. The commercials have to played during the hour they are scheduled for, but the songs are not scheduled for specific times.

So the DJs at WNEW can add and drop songs if they want to without talking to the program director. "I may change five songs in one hour one day, and none the next. Our format allows me to do that," says Carol Miller of WNEW.

DJs have other responsibilities away from the studio. They record commercials for the radio station, promotional announcements, and public service announcements. They also make promotional appearances, since they are the most recognizable people from the station. They may get involved with community activities like a charity softball game against a local team. The DJ sometimes broadcasts from a restaurant with a live audience instead of from the studio.

The DJ's job has changed in the past decade. For years, all music that was played on radio came from either records or tape cartridges, known as *carts*. Then, in 1983, the compact disc was born. Now many radio stations, including WNEW, play most of their music directly from CDs. Most DJs like them because they can get a song ready in an instant. CD players use a laser beam to play the music recorded on the CD, and a DJ can choose a song by pushing a button; to hear song #7, push #7 on the CD player. CDs are also smaller and easier to handle than records, and most people think they sound much better.

Another major change has been in the use of an *engineer* during a show. Until recently, the DJ's only responsibility while on the air was to talk. Getting the records ready to play and running the equipment was done by an engineer. Now, the DJs do it all. Why? Money, basically. In order to save money, radio stations combined the jobs of DJ and engineer. Some DJs like it this way. WNEW's Pat St. John says it makes his show go smoother because if he wants something done, he doesn't have to explain it to someone else. Some shows still use engineers, like the morning shows at both Z-100 and WNEW. They have so much going on—playing music and talking about it, announcing contests and promotions, running commercials, and conducting interviews with live guests—that one person couldn't possibly do it all.

Being a DJ at WNEW and Z-100 are very different jobs because of their formats. On Z-100 the DJs have to be happy and entertaining to listen to. The DJs at WNEW have to be entertaining, but they also have to know about the music being played. DJs from both stations admire the work that the other ones do. "It's hard to be a DJ at a sta-

tion like Z-100. You always have to be entertaining," says Carol Miller of WNEW. Jonathan Bell, a DJ at Z-100, says he sometimes wishes he could work at a station like WNEW. "I sometimes wish I could talk about things I have experienced. But for the people who listen to our station, six months is a long time ago."

Listen carefully to DJs. If they sound like they are sitting in your room having a conversation with you, then you know they are very good at their jobs.

THE BUSINESS

Commercial radio stations don't play music as a public service. Radio is a business. A commercial radio station makes money by selling airtime on the station to advertisers. The people who sell that time work in the *sales department*.

The *general sales manager* runs the sales department. At WNEW, the general sales manager is Jill Colombo. She is responsible for all sales of commercial airtime at the radio station. She has a staff of *sales representatives*, and each of them has different responsibilities.

The *local sales representatives* get new local advertisers for the station. They often call stores and local businesses and try to convince them to buy advertising time on the radio station. About one out of every five businesses say they may be interested. The local sales representative then has to show the store or business owner that by advertising on the radio station he or she will sell more of his or her product or service. That is done by showing the owner what type of person listens to the station and how many people listen to the station each day. The number of people who listen to the station each day is shown by the station's *ratings*. The greater the number of people who listen to the station, the higher the ratings. Say, for example, the owner of a shoe store says she is interested in advertising on WNEW. She says most of her customers are men who are about thirty years old. WNEW is very popular with men that age, so the local sales representative tells the store owner that, and hopes that the owner will buy time on the station to reach them.

The *national sales manager* sells time to big companies with businesses all over the country, like manufacturers of brand name products and large retail stores like Sears. Since the national sales manager can't be all over the country at the same time, stations use *rep companies* to represent them. These companies have offices all over the country, and they sell time for local stations in other cities. Northwest Airlines, headquartered in Minnesota, may want to advertise on New York radio stations like WNEW and Z-100. So Northwest calls the rep company and says it wants to buy time on a New York radio station to which men in their thirties listen. The rep company sells time on WNEW and reports the sale to the national sales manager.

The general sales manager knows how many commercials she has to sell and how much to charge for the radio station to stay in business. Rates are determined by many things, but the most important factors are supply and demand. If there is high demand (many companies and businesses want to buy commercial time) and the supply is low (most commercial time at the station has already been sold), then the station can charge a lot of money for commercial time. However, if only a few companies and businesses want to buy time and the station has a lot of commercial time available, then the station has to lower the price. The actual cost of a minute of commercial time on a radio station depends on many things, including the time of day the advertiser wants the commercial played (a minute of commercial time costs more when more people are listening), the station's ratings, and the station's size.

The sales department often works with other departments to make the radio station more appealing to advertisers. One of those is the *promotions department*, which is run by the *promotions director*. His job is to get more people to listen to the radio station, which means higher ratings, which means more money for commercial airtime.

Radio stations are a little like politicians running for office. Candidates in an election want people to vote for them, so they campaign for votes. They advertise on television and radio, give speeches, and hand out buttons and hats with their names on them. A radio station does similar things; the promotions department runs the campaign.

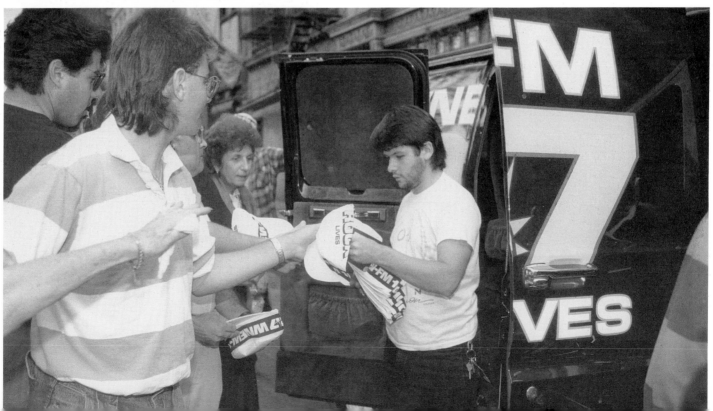

Both WNEW and Z-100 are very successful stations and have a lot of listeners, but each has listeners who like their station more than any other. "Hardly anybody listens to only one radio station all the time. But people have their favorite and that's what we try to be," says WNEW's pro-

motions director, Neil Barry. He and his assistant design promotions to encourage people to listen to the station. Promotions can include contests, concerts, and giveaways at street fairs. Every year, Z-100 holds a Halloween costume contest at a local shopping mall. The promotions department often

asks a disc jockey to make a personal appearance for the station. For example, a DJ may go on stage before a concert to introduce a band. All of these promotional events are designed to make more people aware of the radio station so they will listen to it.

Because WNEW and Z-100 have such different formats, their promotions departments try to get people to listen to the stations in different ways. WNEW does about three hundred promotions a year and some are quite big. They once held a contest and sent the winner to London, England, for a concert. But Z-100 does over one thousand events each year! During the summer, someone from the station goes to every beach and street fair in the area and gives away prizes. If something is happening that will draw a lot of people, there's a good chance Z-100 will be there.

WNEW and Z-100 use their promotions departments in different ways because they have different listeners. People who listen to WNEW often do so because they don't want the flash of a station like Z-100. People who listen to Z-100 want that additional entertainment. Promotions departments design events they think their different audiences will like, and so what works for WNEW would not work as well for Z-100.

The promotions department also creates all advertising for the radio station, including television, newspapers, magazines, and billboards. Again, what works for WNEW would not work as well for Z-100. WNEW's audience is older, so the advertising reflects that. Their ads feature the music played on the station, whereas Z-100 promotes their entertainment, like the "Z Morning Zoo."

The promotions department also works with the *production department*. The production department at any radio station is responsible for the produced sound of the station, which means anything that is not live. That includes commercials, promotional announcements (for example, WNEW is giving away compact discs; with music and sound effects in the background, a voice tells you how to enter the contest), *station IDs* (with sound effects in the background, a recorded voice says, "You're listening to WNEW-FM, the place where rock lives"), and *sweepers* (basically a short station ID that's played in between two songs.)

The production department aims to make all produced pieces of the radio station sound interesting to the listeners. In order to do this, the *production director*, who heads the department, needs to be able to do many things well. He has to write interesting promotional announcements, have a pleasant voice, and be an expert at using the various tape recorders and other machines in the station's studio.

Let's look at a typical job done by the production department from beginning to end. A large sandwich shop in New York buys advertising time on WNEW. Along with the commercial time, the shop wants a promotional giveaway. So the sales department asks the promotions department for an idea. The promotions department suggests that the station give away six-foot submarine sandwiches from the shop, and they ask production director Sal D'Aleo to produce an announcement for it. After thinking about it and trying out different ideas, Sal writes a script and chooses the music and sound effects he wants to use. Then he records the written script on tape. For this particular script, Sal needs two voices: his own, and that of Pat St. John, one of the disc jockeys. After the voices are taped, Sal adds the music and sound effects by playing all three (voices, music, and sound effects) at the same time and recording them onto another tape. Sal then makes sure one part isn't too loud or too soft. If the voices are too loud, people won't hear the music and sound effects. If the music is too loud, people won't hear the script about the sandwich contest. Sal uses a *mixing board* to control the volume of each part individually.

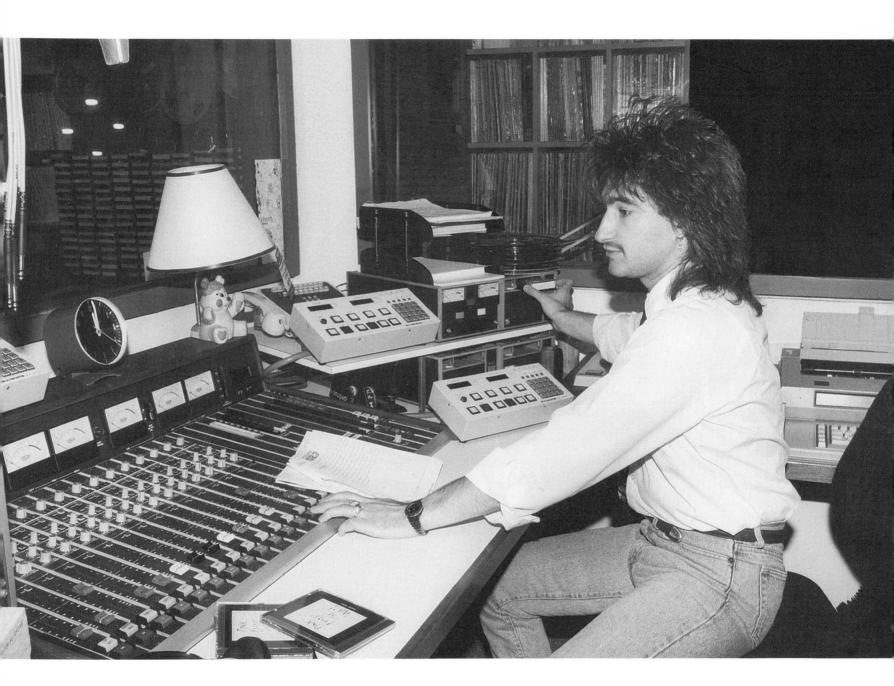

After a few tests, Sal is ready to record the announcement onto a tape cartridge, or cart. A cart is like a big cassette with the tape in a continuous loop. When it is done playing, you don't have to rewind it because it is back at the beginning. Carts come in different lengths; they can be as short as five seconds or as long as nine and a half minutes.

This is how Sal's final version sounds:

Pat: "WNEW, the station that gave you telephone answering machines [drum roll finishing with the crash of a cymbal], compact disc machines [another drum roll and cymbal], and even six-foot sub machines."
Sal: "Uhhh, Pat, that's six-foot submarines."
Pat: "Sal, you didn't taste them" [the sound of a bass drum after a joke: ba-da-bup].

Then music comes on and Pat explains how to win a six-foot submarine sandwich. Sure, Sal could have just written a script saying, "You can win a sandwich by calling this number." It would have been a lot less work—and a lot less interesting.

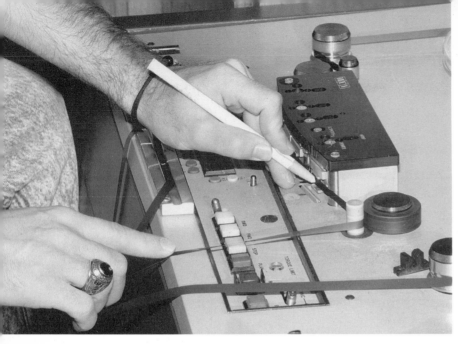

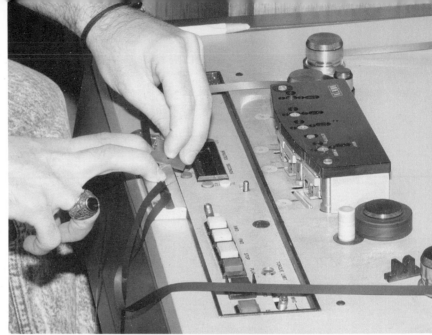

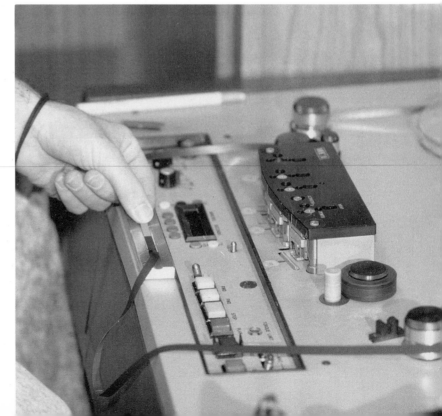

As well as using the mixing board, the production director has to edit audio tape. *Editing* means physically cutting tape with a razor blade and putting it back together in a different order. For example, Pat recorded his part of the script several times. The first time he recorded it, he read his first line very well, but made a mistake on the last part. The second time, though, the last part sounded great but the first line was only fair. So Sal took the first line from the first recording and combined it with the final part of the second recording to make them sound like they were done at the same time.

As I said before, radio is a business. People who own radio stations want to make money. The *business manager* handles the business side of the station and reports to the owner. How much does the radio station spend and earn? Is it making money? Or is it losing money? Every month the business manager talks to all the other department heads to find out how much money they plan to spend that month. Does the production department need a new piece of equipment or does it need to repair something that broke down? Does the promotions department need money for a concert it is putting on at a restaurant? After finding out how much money the station will spend, including things like rent, the electric bill, and employees' salaries, the business manager has a meeting with the sales manager to find out how much money the station has coming in. The business manager also makes sure that all advertisers who buy commercial time on the station pay the station.

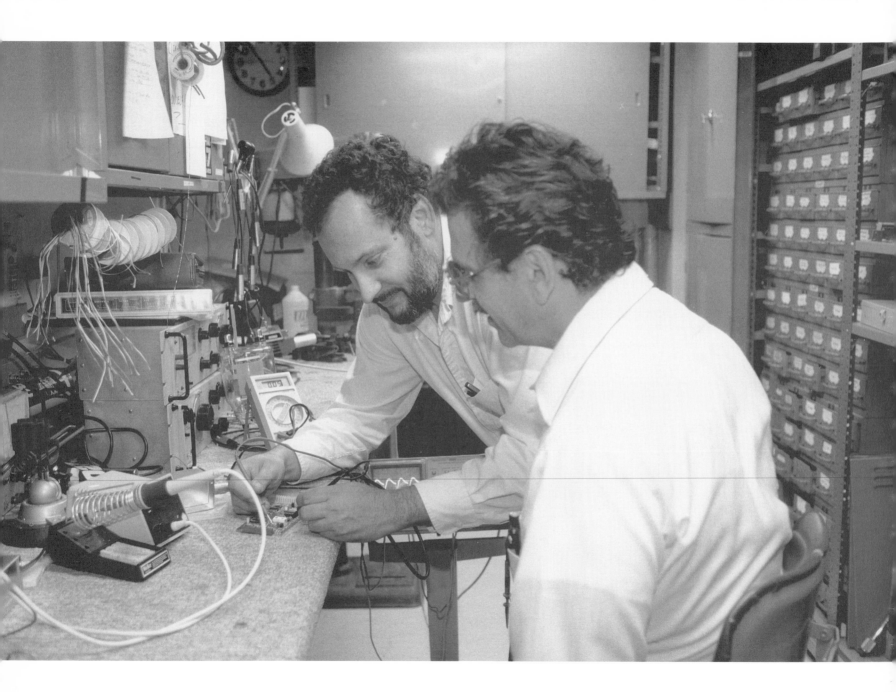

ENGINEERING

You can't run a radio station with people only. A station also needs thousands of dollars worth of fancy electronic equipment (a transmitter, amplifiers, and antennas) to make it work. The people who operate and maintain that equipment work in the *engineering department*, which is headed by the *chief engineer*.

The responsibilities of the engineering department go beyond the electrical equipment at the station. The chief engineer is responsible for researching antenna patterns. All radio stations have big antennas called *transmitting antennas* that send the station's signal for radios to pick up. Theoretically, transmitting antennas should send a signal out in all directions evenly. But sometimes they don't. They may send a signal for two hundred miles in one direction but only twenty-five miles in another. So if a station's antenna is sending its signal two hundred miles out into the ocean and only twenty five miles onto land, not many people are going to be able to hear the station. The chief engineer does research to determine how the signal would change if he were to move the antenna.

Both WNEW and Z-100 have their transmitters at the top of the Empire State Building. Someone from the engineering department goes to the transmitter at least once a week to make sure all of the equipment there is operating properly.

WNEW has a backup transmitter and a backup studio there in case of a power failure at the regular studio.

Along with its technical work, the engineering department does some very important paperwork for a radio station. Every radio station in the country has to keep records for the Federal Communications Commission (FCC). The FCC is the government agency that enforces laws regarding radio and television stations. The records that must be kept include the station's operating power, the sign-on, sign-off log, and the station's public file. Operating power is like a radio transmitter's volume control. The more power, the farther a radio signal can be heard. The FCC tells every station in the country how much power it can operate with. Whenever disc jockeys begin and end their shift they have to sign the *sign-on, sign-off log* because while a radio station is in operation, the FCC says somebody has to be responsible. If somebody forgets to sign the log and the FCC comes to inspect the station, they'll look at the log and think that nobody was operating the station for a period of time. The *public file* contains things like license renewal applications to the FCC (licenses to operate a radio station are good for seven years, after which the owner of the station has to apply to the FCC for a renewal) and reports on equal employment. Anybody can walk into a radio station during normal business hours and ask to see the public file.

The program director and disc jockeys give a radio station its personality, but it is the equipment and the people in the engineering department that put and keep a station on the air so you can hear it.

THE GENERAL MANAGER

The general manager (GM) is the person in charge of the radio station. Everybody else mentioned in this book (except the owner) calls the GM "boss." Most GMs oversee the business end of a radio station, hire and fire staff, and report to the owner on how the station is doing. On top of all that, all department heads at a radio station report to the GM. The GM doesn't tell the program director what music to play or the sales manager how to sell commercial time. Specific decisions are left up to those people, although the GM can offer suggestions.

At both WNEW-FM and Z-100, the GM constantly meets and talks with the different department heads. Once a week, they gather in the GM's office for a staff meeting. The GM usually begins the meeting with some comments about the station's ratings, its sales of commercial time, and anything else that is on his mind. Then he asks all the department heads to talk about what's going on in their departments. Everybody is welcome and encouraged to speak up if they have a question or comment. The GM also has many informal meetings with people who work at the station. His door is almost always open to the people who work there.

The GM reports to the owner on all aspects of the radio station. Because radio is a business, the most important thing to an owner is for the radio station to make money, so sales and other business matters are talked about most frequently. But the owner and the GM do talk about things like programming, promotions, and disc jockeys.

The GM is responsible to the owner for both the station's success and its problems. "GMs take too much credit when things are going well, and too much blame when things are not going well," says Z-100's GM, Gary Fisher. "The people who really make a radio station work are the DJs, the program director, and everybody else that puts us on the air." Maybe, but a good boss makes everybody do his or her job a little bit better.

CONCLUSION

When Guglielmo Marconi obtained his first patent on "wireless telegraphy" in 1896, I doubt he had a WNEW or Z-100 in mind. And I think it is safe to assume that he never planned on his invention broadcasting news twenty four hours a day, or live concerts, or sporting events. But I think he would probably be very happy with radio today. It has something for everybody...and it may even have everything for somebody.

INDEX

Bold page numbers indicate where the definition of a term may be found.